The 15
Map To Booking
H A N D B O O K

The Lyndon
Technique

*A Revolutionary and Practical Approach
to Cold Reading and Booking the Job!*

Created and Written by
Amy Lyndon

I Am Enough, Inc.
Studio City, CA

The Lyndon Technique
The 15 Guideline Map To Booking Handbook
Created and Written by Amy Lyndon

Published and Distributed in the United States by:

TM

I Am Enough, Inc.
11333 Moorpark Street, Suite 458
Studio City, CA 91602
www.coldreadingclasses.com
coldreadingclasses@yahoo.com
818.760.8501

Illustrations, Designs and Handbook Layout by Thomas Garner
Back Cover Photograph by Collin Stark

Printed in the United States of America

Acknowledgments

With deep thanks to my wonderful Thomas for always giving me
unconditional love, support and fantastic notes. My life would
be colorless without your humor and beautiful designs.

Thank you to Mom, Dad, Nunu, Michelle and Jen
for your consistant encouragement.

To my dear students, who encouraged me to write this book.

To Harry Mastrogeorge for teaching me
that story always comes first.

INTRODUCTION

TO BOOK OR NOT TO BOOK – THAT IS THE QUESTION!

Get ready to learn a proven technique to booking the job on the first take. This way of working is for anyone that wishes to compete at a high level. My 15 Guideline Booking Technique is a *"take no prisoners"* way of working and any Actor at any level can use it. It is for those who wish to learn how to break down a script properly and enjoy the ride in the audition room without having a better audition in the car on the way home. Your goal is to go from the bottom 99% to the top 1% of Actors booking jobs. If you want your booking stats to go up, then pay close attention. After perfecting this technique you will be able to pick up any script in any genre and always know what you are doing.

This is not an easy technique, but once you've got it down, you will never forget it. In order for you to absolutely understand how this works, you need to get out there and practice. Audition for anything you can. You don't need to take the job, but you must learn how to book it. This is not an overnight fix. Give it some time and it will all click in. Learn by doing. It's a different way of working. Think of this innovative and practical technique like learning a whole new language.

I believe that I present a unique approach to booking a job and building an acting career because I am out there auditioning and working my business and marketing campaigns alongside all of my students. I have owned and operated a personal management company for nine years, cast several Feature Films, Shorts and Pilots, and have won awards for Acting, Directing, Writing and Producing. I understand what you need to do to succeed. I understand how the energy in the outer casting office and in the audition room can determine your success. I know how difficult it can be. There was a period in my life when I had three survival jobs at one time just to pursue my acting career. I've sold t-shirts at swap meets, waited tables, had an Amway business, made flower arrangements for bar mitzvahs, sold advertising door to door and even got up at 4 o'clock in the morning to sell toner for copy machines from a boiler room phone operation. I know what it takes to make it happen. I have made a ridiculous amount of mistakes along the way and I am thrilled to share my experiences with you to save you the time and heartache.

I moved to Hollywood directly following my college education where I received a BFA in Drama from Syracuse University. When I graduated, I had all this juice flowing and I was so psyched to get out there, but the people in the audition room terrified me because I didn't know what

I was doing. I didn't have a technique or a map to figure out the whole process. I was flying by the seat of my pants. I didn't know how to take all my fantastic training and apply it to booking a job. Slowly over time, I figured out how to book and the biggest thing I learned was that it was never my talent. It was my approach. It's unfortunate, but no one will know how great an Actor you are if your approach is wrong.

These Guidelines will also keep you safe in the room. You will no longer pick up energy from the decision makers or other Actors at the audition because you will be busy setting up your environment, making your opening moment strong in the outer office, telling the story from your point of view, and knowing exactly who you are relating to in the scene. Part of the reason Actors have issues booking is nerves and judgment. You want to act because you have talent and want to be seen, but when you're seen, you're nervous and affected by the judgment of the decision makers. It's sad to think that the main reason why you became an Actor is the same reason why you're not working.

The good news is; those days are over! I am giving you a map to booking so you will always know exactly what you are doing. You will get to a place where you'll be so completely immersed with the story and the specifics that you won't have time to be nervous. It won't even matter who's in the room at that point because you'll be too busy. You will go in, hit the audition hard, walk to your car and before you know it, you had an amazing experience and you won't even remember who was in the room. THAT is the ultimate goal we all strive for!

With this technique, **you cannot skip corners and be lazy**. Answer the questions in the order that it is laid out in this handbook. Remember, you are only going to be as good as your homework. Write the answers to the questions directly onto the pages of your script. If it's not written all over the pages, then it's going to be in your head. The more homework you do, the more specific you're going to be, and the more you're going to be able to completely let go and perform at the top of your game. This is a tedious and logically straightforward technique that requires great discipline, but it is worth it when you see the results. You can literally turn your career around today. It really is true that, *"Success occurs when pre-paredness meets opportunity."*

G U I D **1** E L I N E

WHAT IS THE SCENE ABOUT?

When you receive your "sides" also known as a "scene" or "script" for an audition, read it 10 times and ask yourself, *"In one sentence, what is this scene about?"* Write it on the top of the sides. The sentence needs to be from the storytelling point of view. The more time you spend outside of the scene, as a reader, like you're seven years old reading a book for the first time, the better off you're going to be. Describe the scene in one sentence. For example, *"A man and woman argue about the wedding of a close friend."* If you jump in too quickly, then you'll have no perspective on what's really going on in the story. You're only going to be playing what you think you should be playing instead of understanding the whole story from the Writer's perspective. A great example would be a catchphrase on a movie poster that says, *"She conquered, he made love mercifully, they were a frightful pair."* Make sure the sentence is not from your point of view. It needs to be from the story's point of view.

The story ALWAYS comes first. The Writer is the captain of the ship. Respect the Writer. You don't get the opportunity to re-write the script to fit your needs. Whatever the Writer tells you to do, do it. You're the Actor, not the Writer or the Director. The sides will tell you everything you need to know. **DON'T MAKE ANYTHING UP.** What you are reading is the truth. If the character says that they hate the other person, then they hate the other person in that moment until it changes - unless there's an action line or a parenthetical suggesting otherwise. Don't make anything up to make your read stand out to impress anyone. You will stand out if you read it exactly as written. **THE WRITER MAKES YOUR "CHOICES" FOR YOU.** Believe me, making random "choices" is the biggest mistake an Actor can make. You want the Writer in the room to say, *"That Actor read it exactly as I wrote it - that's the character!"* It's not a mystery when the Casting Director says, *"That's the girl! She's exactly as I saw her."* And the Director says, *"That's the girl! She's exactly as I need her to be."* That is what happens when you read it exactly as written. Take the time to figure out the Writer's intent. **THIS IS THE KEY TO GETTING INTO THE 1%.**

Remember when we were little kids in school? The teacher would point to each kid and say, *"You're going to be a gum tree, you're going to be the fairy princess, and you're going to be the pumpkin"* and we would excitedly say, *"Okay."* There was never an argument; there was never a thought about it. If the Writer wants you to do something, do it. Always ask yourself, *"What does the Writer want me to do today?"* Do it as written. Stop making decisions. Stop deciding how you are going to do it when the script already told you what you are doing.

Don't waste time making up events that are not written. You really do have enough to play with. You don't need to make up a "back story" because it was probably already shot in another scene. Concentrate on the scene at hand. Look at it like a frame in a film. Read everything slowly - including the action. Reading it 10 times will keep you outside of the scene instead of making choices and decisions about your character, which can oftentimes leave out so many details about who you are. It's important to look at each character's point of view without judgment. Because if you don't, you won't be aware of what other people are saying about you and you won't figure out why you're even in the story to begin with. Ask yourself, why did the Writer write you? Why are you in the scene?

Finding the one sentence that describes what the scene is about is the most difficult process of all the guidelines and it cannot be rushed. It takes the longest to figure out. You cannot let yourself go onto the rest of the guidelines without an answer to this question. The story is your foundation. If you don't understand the story, then you cannot be in the story.

If you have a tendency to get adjusted a lot in the room or you get a basic *"That was nice, thanks for coming in"* - chances are you're not in the story as written. You want to go in, nail it, and go home and get on with your life.

Television is story driven. It's very important to know why you're in the script. There are a lot of people who don't book jobs because they're doing too much for the character as written. If you're not the Series Regular, then your main function is to move the story along. Fulfill the story. A lot of Actors want so much to be remembered that they overshoot the audition by becoming more important than the star. Don't pull focus. Know your place in the script. If you're not booking Television, then you think you're more important than the story. For example, if you're serving drinks in the scene, then you're just a cocktail waitress. If you're delivering pizza, then you're just the pizza delivery guy. That's it.

Feature Film on the other hand, is character driven. Every single role in a Feature Film is important. You can receive an Academy Award for a small supporting role. Know why your character is important to the story. Then fulfill the character to the best of your ability.

It is vitally important not to jump in right away and cast yourself. I know you're excited, but you're doing yourself a huge disservice if you jump in too quickly and only look at your lines and make all these decisions aka "choices." If you do that, then you'll only know 50% of the story, your 50%, and therefore only have a 50% chance of booking. When you read both roles equally, you'll have a stronger foundation and understanding 100% of the time.

Be careful of judging the material negatively. When you say things like, *"That would never happen"* or *"That's stupid"* or *"This is written like crap,"* you will never be able to fully immerse yourself inside the scene because you are standing outside of the material. You're putting your focus in the wrong direction. You will never book with that approach. You need to accept that you are simply a clean vessel of pure emotion lending yourself to the material to channel the character from the Writer's intent.

As long as it is according to the Writer's intent you will never be wrong; you will always be in truth. The script will tell you everything you need to know. The story always comes first. You are interesting enough. You don't need to add anything extraneous. You are already different by virtue of the simple fact that there is only one you. Doing the story as written actually gives you more room to bring in your own personality. Just be careful not to let your personality overshadow the character and story as written. Fit yourself into the confines of the story and not the other way around.

It's very important to note that a scene hardly ever starts at the beginning. We're usually dumped into the middle of a conversation that already has the energy within that relationship created. It's your job to bring that energy into the room with you and keep it going. Also, when you are given several scenes, you need to look at each one as different emotional facets of your character. A Casting Director would never waste their time by giving you two of the same emotional types of scenes.

BREAK DOWN THE SCENE INTO A BEGINNING, MIDDLE AND END

Every story has a Beginning, Middle and End. Still standing outside of the story as the reader, figure out the journey your character takes. Your job as a "STORYTELLER" is to take us on that journey. If you don't have a Beginning, Middle and End, you will most definitely flat line. You need to take us from one experience to another.

The way to figure out the breaks between the beginning, middle and end is to analyze when the story or information shifts. The transition can take place on an action line or a parenthetical and always on the literal shift of information according to the story.

Sometimes your "BEGINNING" will just be 2 lines of dialogue. It's also fine that your "MIDDLE" be a huge portion of the scene and the "END" just a handful of dialogue or visa versa. It's whenever the story changes and breaks.

It's important to write "BEGINNING", "MIDDLE" and "END" on the script. You can also draw a line across the page for direct differentiation. It's smart to do that because you need to be reminded to make sharp strong transitions. Strong transitions create strong dynamics in a scene.

Trust that by playing the Beginning, Middle and End in sequence, you will reach where you need to get to at the end of your script. Each section of the story builds on the previous section.

By breaking down the script this way, it will keep you from playing the end of the scene at the beginning. By playing the end of the scene at the beginning, not only are you not telling a story, you are playing a result and giving a one-note performance.

WHAT IS THE CHARACTER'S EMOTIONAL STATE OF MIND AT THE TOP?

Your emotional state of mind has to be in place before you even open your mouth. 90% of your work is done before you walk in the door. The reason why I say that is because if you don't have 90% of your work done before you walk in the door, the rest of your time will be spent running after the emotions in the scene. If your emotional state of mind is not in place, you will play the emotion and not feel it. And if you don't feel it, neither will anyone else watching you. Find out where your opening emotion is for you. If it is "distraught," hook into your emotional reservoir and find out where "distraught" is for you.

This is the jump off point and FOUNDATION for 90% of the scene. If your opening emotion is weak, then you will pick up the energy in the room, fall out in the middle of the scene and spiral down from there. You need to be setting up your opening emotion outside in the waiting room. If you are still breaking down the scene in the waiting room, then you didn't do enough homework. Only concentrate on your emotional state of mind at the top. This will carry you throughout the entire scene. When you throw yourself into the opening emotion, the chances of taking in anything counter to the story is nill.

You need to relate on a DEEP PERSONAL LEVEL! For example, if you've never been a drug addict, how are you going to play one? What do drug addicts go through? Let's talk about withdrawal - have any of you not eaten for a while, became light headed and felt like you were going to bite someone's head off? I know that's a little extreme, but that's how a drug addict feels when they go through withdrawal. In order to fully understand their emotional state of mind you would need to multiply it by 1000. Sit with each feeling and find it. It's the feeling that needs to be found. Not the situation. You need to find the situation whereby you felt that way, locate the button inside you that connects to that feeling, then meditate and rehearse that button. The situation will take you out of the story. The emotion will not. You can take something small and build it up within yourself until it becomes really big. You've got to sell it to yourself so that you can sell it to someone else. But if you don't understand how to connect to the emotions of a drug addict, then you're not going to embody it. Find it, feel it.

Find out why a person is behaving a certain way. If you

understand that, then you'll understand the person. ***If you do not understand your character, you cannot play the character.*** Get out of your head and into your heart. Do whatever you need to do to understand the character, even if it takes you all day asking yourself questions like, *"Why would I do that? Why would I kill my father?"* **Always ask yourself, *"WHY?"*** In this case you might ask yourself these questions, *"How did he hurt me? Maybe I'm feeling abandoned. Maybe he abused me. Where is abandonment for me? Have I ever been abused? Where is abuse and hurt for me emotionally?"* You need to dig deep within yourself because you have to understand the exact emotion. Why should I buy it if you don't buy it? Find that opening emotion and create the discipline to set it in place before you begin your read. Do not start until it is in place. The house will fall without the foundation. When it falls you'll feel all the holes in your work and you are sure to pick up the energy in the room. Throw yourself into the scene! Before you know it, you'll be done and in your car asking yourself, *"What just happened?"* That's an amazing feeling.

GUID 4 LINE

MAP OUT YOUR EMOTIONS

From your character's perspective, what are his/her emotions in the Beginning, Middle and End of the story? If this is not clear, expect to lose your audience with your one-dimensional performance. Sit with each feeling in each section until it becomes a deep connected one. If you're having trouble connecting, close your eyes and locate a similar feeling you can connect with and lay the line on top. Ask yourself, *"What am I feeling? WHAT AM I REALLY FEELING?"*

NEVER RUN LINES! JUST FEELINGS! If you run lines, it will sound like lines run. But if you run thoughts, you will always be in the moment. The moment you relate on a deep personal level is the moment your audience becomes attached to your performance. Have you ever been involved with one thing and wanted to do something else, like kissing someone? Can you relate to that on a deep personal level? Once you relate on a deep personal level, it's easy to play. There is nothing else going on but that feeling. We don't want to see the whole movie in that moment. We don't even want to see the whole scene in that moment. We just want to see the moment. It's a domino effect. If you don't set the first emotion in motion during the beginning, then it's not going to lead and build upon the next one and the next one. So, fulfill each moment to the fullest and don't bother thinking about anything other than the moment that you're in. Don't direct it. Feel it. How do you expect your audience to be surprised if it's directed? Take them on your emotional journey from one moment to the next. Great acting equals great moments.

It has always amazed me when I see notes on an Actor's script that read "Sarcastic" or "Funny" or "Serious." Those are Directorial values. Definitely not hooked into any type of feeling. You're sure to be in your head and not your heart when you write down results instead of feelings.

Always ask yourself, *"Where is this for me? How can I relate to this?"* For example, a parenthetical states "(feigning interest)." Ask yourself, *"Where is feigning interest for me? How do I behave when I feign interest? Do I even know what feigning interest is? What do I do when I feign interest? How do I feel when I feign interest? Do I even understand what a feigning interest feeling is?"* If you don't understand it, you can't play it! Be specific with your understanding of character. Do the research. If you understand the character and the character's feelings you will be the character and there will be no questions asked because you will say with enormous conviction, *"I can do this because I know exactly who this person is."* And guess what, *that person* will be walking into the audition room.

All you want anyone to say is, *"That's the guy we're looking for!"* or *"That's the girl we're looking for!"* That's it! All they want to know is, did you hit the emotional notes? Did you **represent** that character as written? Are you the guy? Are you the girl? You will be MORE the guy and MORE the girl, based on how your character feels.

Don't forget, the opening emotion is 90% of the entire scene. It is the foundation. If it's not strong you will be chasing after it throughout the entire scene and probably fall out in the middle. If your opening emotion is strong, nothing is going to bother you. The phone ringing, the Casting Director's state of emotion, and people talking loudly into their cell phones won't penetrate your zone because you are in the emotional life of the character. You also won't be thinking about your car payment or the house you're going to buy when you book the job. When your opening emotion is strong, you will stay focused.

You have to relate on a deep personal level! Let's say the

character is going through a divorce and she's on her way to see her ex, what does that feel like? I'd rather you spend the entire car ride and the entire time in the waiting room feeling that, than running the scene. If you run the scene, it will flatten out and you will never grab them at the top. But if you come in with the raw emotion of what's really happening at this time with this person, then you will grab them immediately. The moment you walk through the door they know whether or not you're in the running. Trust me, I've cast projects before. The first 30 seconds will determine whether you are in or out.

MAJOR NOTE: *I am speaking of the emotional life RIGHT NOW! Not the history; the present. Don't worry about "the back story" because you're not playing that.*

If you have trouble locating and switching emotions quickly, exercise your emotions on a daily basis. Pick an emotion, let's say "fear", locate where fear is for you and sit with it until it becomes a 'button' that you can push for yourself, and then journal where it is for you for future use. Find out where each emotion is located in your body so that you can easily tap into it at a moments notice. There are tons of emotions to choose from. You might not find it in a day. Meditate on it until you do find it. You are an instrument that needs to be practiced every day. Always remember, the only difference between a good

Actor and a brilliant Actor is depth of feel.

Don't blow by the emotional descriptions. If it says, *"A tear drops,"* the person that drops that tear with 100% commitment is going to win the job. The Actor that goes the emotional distance, according to the story, gets the most toys.

Let's say your Agent sends you out for a stripper role. First of all, don't make a judgment on a stripper's lifestyle. Instead, ask yourself *"Why is somebody a stripper? What kind of person is a stripper? Do I know any strippers? What is a stripper's lifestyle? How am I going to understand stripping?"* Playing an idea or a concept of a stripper, will never in a million years book you the role of a stripper, because you don't understand it. Someone else will come into that audition and embody the stripper emotionally and will take your job.

The truth is, you could dress like a stripper, and you might be that great and fool them and maybe they don't have any better choices, but I'm saying if you want to secure a booking, do the specific emotional homework. Do the research.

STUDENT: *What about a housewife who has a drug and drinking problem?*

AMY: *Have you personally ever had a drug or drinking problem?*

STUDENT: *No.*

AMY: *So, how are you going to relate to it emotionally? You've got to dig deep and ask questions.*

STUDENT: *Well, she has emotional needs. Is that the place where you would go to connect to the character?*

AMY: *Yes. Exactly. What are a housewife's emotional needs? To secure the booking, you would first have to understand why she's a drug addict and alcoholic to begin with. Everything has a reason. Keep asking, "WHY?"*

STUDENT: *She's lonely. Her husband is never home and it says here that she feels like a loser and good for nothin'.*

AMY: *Have you ever felt like a loser and good for nothin'?*

STUDENT: *Yeah.*

AMY: Great place to start. *Sit with it until you can locate that exact button for you. Rehearse the button and go deeper each time.*

The more you get underneath the emotions and look at the specifics and understanding of it, rather than the face value, the more your performance will lift to this whole other level and you will see your booking statistics rise.

Most of your time as an Actor needs to be spent meditating and dreaming about specific emotions. Just sit with it and dig within and ask yourself *"Where is this for me? Where can I relate to this within myself?"* Keep digging until you find it. Pick any emotion. "Devastation" for example: ask yourself, *"Have I ever been completely devastated?"* You have to pick the most extreme devastation. It can't be just devastation at 5. It's got to be devastation at 10. When you get to the core of the emotion you will know it. Push your own buttons. Whenever we're upset, happy, angry, sad, etc. we do it to ourselves. We push our own buttons. When I saw "Mystic River," I truly believed that Sean Penn was DEVASTATED. Absolutely devastated. He was devastated at 10+. That's why he won the Academy Award for "Best Actor" that year.

When you really connect to the character's exact emotion, you will feel the room move forward. You will never be boring. You will always be interesting to watch.

When I was casting ODESSA (a movie that I wrote, directed and produced), I had several people who came in for the role of "Odessa." There was this one woman who came in and she was exactly as I envisioned the character of "Odessa." She was a big woman with a big bosom and I had always felt that the little girl in the story would lie on that bosom and feel protected. She also had a resume with a substantial amount of theatre and I have a huge respect for theatre Actors – since I was one myself. I've got to say, she played the crap out of it. Then Yolanda King (Dr. Martin Luther King Jr's eldest daughter) came in. She wasn't physically how I wrote "Odessa," but Yolanda King embodied the role of "Odessa." She understood the pain and essence of the character and she had an inherent sense of loss. She was "Odessa." The other woman played "Odessa." That's the difference you need to understand.

This step needs to be taken seriously because if you come in with a strong emotion and strong understanding of where the character is emotionally coming from, your chances of booking increases substantially. You need to have the essence and soul of the character you play.

The beginning emotion can encompass one line to several paragraphs. The beginning emotion needs to stay with you until the emotion changes into the middle and then changes again into the end. Mark each emotional change and work those emotions and transitions from one emotion to another. Don't run them together. Work in sections. Separate them out and rehearse each emotion until you've got it located deep within you and locked down. When it comes audition time, set it up, let it go, and enjoy the ride.

G U I D **5** L I N E

WHAT IS THE KEY LINE?

The key line is the character's emotional spine and through line. The key line can be found in your dialogue or the other character's dialogue. It's not always easy to find. You need to look for it.

Knowing the key line will keep you on-point through out the scene and it will keep you focused on what you're trying to say or not say. We all have a secret agenda going on when we speak with someone. We're always thinking about something when we listen to what the other person is saying.

Look at the key line as a summation to your story. It could be a line like, *"I have always loved him."* The key line is your anchor.

READ THE ACTION
IN IT'S ENTIRETY

The action supports the emotional work and tells you what you are doing and what is happening in the scene. Since Film and Television are visual mediums, you have to "factor in" or "do the action" so the story has movement. If you're only going to look at your dialogue and the other character's dialogue and not look at the long lines that describe the action, you're cheating yourself out of the movement in the story. The action can actually help you get the job because most people don't pay attention to it. So, if it says *"Interior Renaldo's Gallery – Night"* pay attention. The *"Night"* is what gives you the texture and/ or tone and *"Interior Renaldo's Gallery"* is what tells you what you might be doing. The brilliance is in the specifics. Keep in mind that everyone auditioning is bad, good or great. But what makes an Actor brilliant is their attention to detail. Action is a major detail and must be paid serious respect.

"A swinging art gallery jammed" - gives you more information. What does this tell you? It tells you that you

have to visualize a jammed art gallery and what it's like to be in a place that is filled to the brim with people. *"People with plastic cups filled with wine"* – okay, they're drinking. *"Zoey is pacing in the crowd, one of the few not wearing black"* – they're all wearing black so what kind of a crowd is it? Upscale, downtown New York maybe? Keep asking questions. Maybe it has that artsy, nouveau 'everybody is a critic' kind of feel. This information is important! The action is indicating how you are going to dress and feel in the environment. If you are "Zoey," then you're not wearing black. Could you possibly not belong there? She's "pacing." Does she feel out of place? Is it because of what she's wearing? This gives you the tone of the environment. The action needs to be fleshed out specifically because part of the reason why some of you don't book is because you pick up the energy in the room. The place (environment) will keep you safe and busy. The story and state of mind of the character as indicated by action keeps your nerves at bay. You can create the "jammed" feel and not move anywhere in the office. Just feel it.

Circle action. Action will tell you what you are doing because you'll know exactly what is happening in the scene. The action will help you set up the movement, which will pop the scene and create the illusion as if you are transported into the character's world. You can include action in your audition, however if the script tells you that the character is making a sandwich but the dialogue is not indicating anything about the sandwich, do not make a sandwich in your audition. If you are drunk and drinking wine, then mime drinking wine. Only do this if there is mention about your drinking or drunk behavior in the script and you are downing wine like a fiend. If you put in action when it's not mentioned then you'll only be a distraction to yourself and the people in the room. If you choose to do the action, then choreograph it ahead of time. Don't at the last minute incorporate the action at your audition and surprise yourself with it because it will throw you out of the scene. If you don't do the action, then factor it into the dialogue. For example, if you're not going to hold a drink, yet according to the script your character has been drinking, figure out how much and incorporate it into the dialogue. Are you slurring? How much? Falling down drunk? How much alcohol has your character consumed? Do the specific research.

I AM NOT TALKING ABOUT MIMING YOUR WAY THROUGH YOUR SCENE! But, if the action says, *"Johnny opens the door abruptly,"* then if you're playing Johnny, you have to open the door abruptly and that abruptness would indicate how your character is feeling at the top of the scene. If you were playing the person on the other side of the door, then you would need to factor in that abruptness into your opening emotion. Certainly if a door was opened abruptly in my face, I would flinch to say the least. That abrupt action indicates what emotional state the other character is going through and what you're going to be dealing with on the other side.

Action can also be helpful in creating physical movement. If the action says, *"Susan is waiting impatiently for Chad to arrive."* How would she be sitting at the table in the restaurant? Would she be playing with her napkin? Would she be looking around? Would she be checking her face? Her watch? How would Susan behave? Work it out.

If the action indicates that you're in the emergency room in the hospital with a burnt hand for six hours, how would the action help your state of mind? First of all, it must be a bad burn to go to the emergency room to begin with and it's got to be getting worse by the hour. How much is your hand throbbing? How would you be holding your hand? Where exactly is the pain located? How is this pain affecting your mood? What is it like to be waiting for six hours in excruciating pain? What would you be doing while you are waiting? Would you be sitting or standing in front of the check-in desk staring at the lady behind the desk disapprovingly? Think it through. Ask the questions.

The action is especially important in physical comedy because it will give you the physicality, which oftentimes sets up the comedic situation. If you don't read the action you won't know what's going on because the action could be setting up the joke. That's why sitcom is situational comedy. How does the action set up the situation?

Never bring any props to your audition unless it's already on you like a cell phone or a pen. Always remember that the stronger the illusion you create in the room, the better the ride for you and the people watching you.

EVERY LINE IS
A SEPARATE THOUGHT

Go over every single line and write down what you are saying in your own words next to each line. Some people might relate to this as "subtext." Sit with each line until you understand it from the WRITER'S PERSPECTIVE. Ask yourself, ***"What am I saying? What am I REALLY saying?"*** If you don't know what you're saying, figure out what the other character just said to you. This will clear up how you might respond.

Actors have a tendency to go right to memorizing dialogue because they feel that when it's memorized, they'll then be able to do the work. That's absolutely the opposite way to work. If you break down dialogue and know what you're talking about, the dialogue will miraculously be memorized. If you study or try to memorize lines, then you will forget lines, because that's all it is and it's not connected to anything. Study each piece of dialogue and understand why the next dialogue comes next. You never have to memorize the dialogue because it'll make perfect sense why the next line comes next. When we speak, we speak in a stream of conscious with one thought following another in direct succession. If Actors are there to mirror the truth of life, doesn't it make logical sense to deliver the dialogue in that way?

If you focus on the line, you'll always lose the line. Focus on the understanding of what it is you're saying. Make sure you understand how each line is connected. Even if the script is bad, there is always a reason why the next line comes next. Embrace every line. You do not have any business going onto the next line without fully understanding what you are really saying from the character's perspective. Trust me, if your line isn't filled with exact truth, you will lose your audience. Casting and Producers will space out during your read because you haven't captured their attention with the exact truth. Don't memorize the dialogue and say, *"Okay, I got it."* No, you don't "got it!" Just because you memorized the lines, doesn't mean you understand the lines! Mean what you say and say what you mean!

This one student was giving a great performance and then all of a sudden I dropped out of his scene and I said, *"What were you talking about there because I just got pulled out of the scene?"* He said, *"You know, I really have no idea."* I exclaimed, *"Well, you know what? Neither do I. It's funny how that happens."* I'm telling you, the people that watch your performance don't understand why they're pulled out of the scene. They really don't care or think twice about it. You've subtly lost their attention. They won't know that it's because of one word or one line or one paragraph. They'll throw it off to, *"He/ She is just not right for the role."* The truth is, it's always when you haven't a clue what you are talking about. And it's not a question of running it and running it and running it. It's a question of going over each line and asking yourself, "Do I really know what I'm saying from my very being, from my very soul?"

Don't write down next to the line how you're going to do it like, "flirty" or "obnoxious" because that's a value, not an understanding of what you are saying. Every line has to be a separate thought. Write down your true thoughts aka "subtext" next to each line. Don't use the same words that are already in the dialogue. If you do that then you are rewriting instead of really sitting with each line and understanding it to the fullest. You want to get underneath the dialogue. You don't want to be working on the surface by directing how you're going to be saying your line. Repeating your lines in different ways until you think you've hit the right way to say it is not the way to break down dialogue.

You can literally spend ten minutes breaking down each

line of dialogue. If you know exactly what you're saying then the line will basically read itself. When you get more specific with your thoughts, the line will come out perfect. It will be smooth, like butter. Don't practice your lines. Practice your thoughts. Make sure your thoughts are really clear and specific. Practice what you're really saying and then lay the line on top. If you're going to rehearse, rehearse thoughts, not the lines. If you run lines, it will appear to be lines run. It will be flatter than a pancake.

Believe it or not, it's all there. The Writer has already given you the map. You have to look for the answers and practice the thoughts and feelings according to the Writer's intent. The character's thoughts are already written for you. Figure them out and understand them deep inside you.

DON'T CLUMP! If there's a paragraph of dialogue, don't give a value or one line for the 18 lines that appear in front of you. You need to break down all 18 lines into a clear understanding of what you are saying. Thoughts change. Do you continue with the same thoughts with everything that you say? Why should it be any different when you're acting? Don't be lazy. If you want to be brilliant, you have to do the work.

Punctuation is extremely important. Never ignore punctuation! You need to go over every single question mark, exclamation mark, comma and period. By the way, just because there's an exclamation mark doesn't mean you are yelling. An exclamation mark simply suggests that there is an intense feeling.

Punctuation is key. If you have ever written anything in your life, you would know that by ignoring the punctuation, you're ignoring how the character speaks. The Writer painstakingly goes over and over the punctuation to punctuate the feelings of the character. If you throw out punctuation then every role you play will be the same. There is a ridiculous amount of Actors today that throw out the character's punctuation to accommodate their own language. The Writer needs you to play the role as written. If you want to book more, understand that this isn't brain surgery. Keep it simple. Read it as it is written and understand why it is written that way. By ignoring punctuation you will end up gliding from one thought to another. This will ultimately create a flat performance. You don't want to flatline. You need to hit it, not glide it. If you want to be an interesting Actor, go over every moment and detail and cover it with deep understanding. Every line is like a note in a song. Listen for the music.

Let's cover "Beat." A Beat is not a pause. A beat is filled with the character's thoughts, which leads to a transition

– a new direction in the story or scene.

Another thing to look for when reading the text for story is the physical punctuation. A double dash (--) or an ellipsis (...) during the dialogue like, *"I... I... don't... know if I can do that."* means the character is reaching for words. This can oftentimes be an indication that the character is emotional, nervous or shy. If there's a double dash or an ellipsis at the end of dialogue, the other character is cutting off the person. That can be an indication that the person cutting them off has something important to say and they don't want the other person to finish their thoughts. You have to analyze it and understand why. If you don't understand it, why should anyone else? Understand everything you read at 100%!

The strongest example regarding the importance of punctuation is reflected in comedy. In comedy, the punctuation will tell you how to find the joke. If you glide through the punctuation, the comedy will quickly become a drama. In drama, the punctuation indicates the tone and the character's emotional state of mind. It lets us know how the character feels and speaks.

Also pay careful attention to the parentheticals. If there are a lot of parentheticals, then the Writer doesn't trust that the Actor will understand where the character is coming from emotionally. Some parenthetical examples: (confused), (angry), (suddenly afraid), (jumping up and down) - I know, sometimes scripts are filled with them, but they are warranted because the parenthetical truly specifies the character's emotional state of mind in that moment with that line. If you read it exactly as written, then it would make perfect sense for the Writer to think you are the character "as written" for their project.

Every script you pick up is like a puzzle. The clues to your character are in each and every line. You have to figure it out. You have to put all the pieces together. Did you know that most of your character information could be found in the other character's dialogue? So don't rush when you get a script. Enjoy figuring out the puzzle. The truth is, someone is going to come in and nail it because they will have spent more time understanding the meaning of each line.

G U I D **8** L I N E

WHAT ARE YOU DOING?

Figure out what your character is doing in the beginning, middle and end of the scene. Technically, what you are doing can be a physical action in the scene like, *"I'm entering the house in a hurry, then I'm throwing the door open to my bedroom, then I'm going to catch my girlfriend in bed with the neighbor."* Or, it can be, *"I'm arguing on the phone with my boyfriend and then hang up right before I enter the tennis court, then I'm going to explain why I'm late and plead with the coach for forgiveness, get angry because he cut me from the team, and then I'm going to turn to the team who is staring at me, and yell at them."*

Break it down, break it down, and break it down - into teeny tiny pieces. Knowing what you are doing is like a protective barrier against all the breathing in the room. If you're picking up that energy, then you're really not doing enough homework. Choreograph it like it's a dance routine. Visualize it. Walk it through. Know where you are going and what you are doing in the office. Play the movie in your mind. This does not mean you're directing it, it just means you have to ask yourself, *"How are they going to shoot it? Where's the focus of the scene? What is my character physically doing?"* If you do not know what you are doing, then you're not ready to audition. Knowing what you're doing will give you an incredible amount of confidence.

I am often asked, *"What about kissing?"* With kissing you have to recreate the moment of what it feels like when someone is kissing you even though you're sitting in the middle of a small office in a chair with the Casting Director behind the desk reading. As Actors, you're magicians. You've got to take your audience on a journey into your illusion, and onto your magic carpet ride. Make sure if you're feeling a kiss on the back of your neck, that it's at 100%. Never just "sort of" do anything. Do it all the way. Why should your audience go to ten if you only hit it at five? But, if you go to ten and you're REALLY doing it, REALLY feeling it, believe me, the Casting Director and your audience are going to feel uncomfortable. The deal with intimacy is to make everyone watching feel as if they shouldn't be watching because it's that private. Trust me, if you're not going to go there first, they're not going to follow. Let go and enjoy.

If you don't know what you're doing, then you will appear insecure in the room. Knowing what you are doing will give you the confidence you need to go after the job.

Since we're in such an unstable business, it's important to note that Casting Directors, Writers and Producers don't want to worry about you on the set. They have enough to deal with. If you come off lost or wishy washy, you are sure to get thrown to the bench as "green" or *"not what we're looking for"* or *"we've decided to go in another direction."* They don't want to help you figure it out or take care of you. It's an "add water and stir" business. They need to know that after they hire you, they won't get a call from production asking for their job because you didn't know what you were doing. People hire people who are confident with their work and know what they are doing at all times.

FIND THE TRANSITIONS

The sharper the transition, the better we understand your character. Don't be afraid of transitions. We transition every day in our lives, but we prefer to call them "mood swings." Take a day and notice how many times you switch from one mood to another. Why should it be any different when you act? If you want to be considered interesting and exciting, work your transitions. Your audience will be curious as to what you're going to do next. You want to keep them on their toes. They shouldn't know where you're going. Check out the Actors we consider great. Look at how sharp their transitions are. They paint dynamic beautiful pictures.

We will always understand character because of character transitions. If you're playing a character that transitions at every line, then you're most likely playing a schizophrenic, or a psychologically disturbed person or someone that is highly neurotic that needs Prozac, or someone who drank ten Red Bulls, or is a snitch. Or maybe you're just a character that has a lot to convey in a small amount of time. Either way, you need to have an answer as to why your character transitions so often in a short period of time. The answers are all in the story.

Don't glide transitions because then it becomes a muddled mess. Let's say the character starts out nice, and then they become aggravated, and then they become angry. Don't glide into nice, don't glide into aggravated, and don't glide into angry. HIT it. You've got to hit it hard because someone else will.

It's like when you play tennis and switch grips for your backhand. If you rush it, the ball goes into the net or out of the court because your hand is not locked in place. It's the same thing for emotional transitions. Don't rush emotional transitions. You have to set them up. If they're not in place you're sure to deliver an uninteresting, casual reality performance and lose the game.

HOW DO YOU HEAR WHAT THE OTHER PERSON IS SAYING?

Write down next to each of the other character's lines how you hear what they are saying from your character's point of view. This will keep you focused and active. You will not be thinking about your next line and you'll be invested in the scene. Here's a typical conversation:

                    GIRL
        You're not hearing what I'm saying!
        What I'm saying is, every time you
        look at Sally that way, she thinks
        you're interested.

                    GUY
        No, that's not what you said. You
        told me to stop lusting after your
        sister.

                    GIRL
        That's not what I said.

                    GUY
        Yes. You did. You think I want Sally.

                    GIRL
I said that if you look at her that
way, she will think you want to get
together with her!

                    GUY
You're acting like a jealous
girlfriend.

                    GIRL
No. I'm not. I'm embarrassed and I
don't want her to get the wrong idea.

And the fight continues. The Guy hears the Girl's point
of view as a jealous girlfriend over-reacting and the Girl
hears the Guy's point of view as his avoidance to the issue
of sending the wrong message to her sister.

Your character hears what the other character is saying
based on your character's point of view. **It's not how
the other character is saying it. It's what the other
character is saying and how your character hears
it.** By working this way, you will not pick up the Casting Director's or anyone else's energy and you won't be
concerned with how they are reading. This is also a great
way to get "off book." By hearing what the other person
is saying from your character's point of view, it will make
perfect sense why your line comes next.

Be careful not to do the other character's homework. Do not break down their script. Do your own. Write down next to each of their lines what they are saying from your character's point of view. Don't rewrite their lines. Really think about how your character hears it. This will keep you invested in the scene. You'll be busy listening.

Do you realize that most of the clues to your character is in the other person's dialogue? It's also important to understand what they are saying about you so that you can justify it in your actions and behavior. If the other person says, *"You're acting awfully touchy."* Then you should be "acting awfully touchy" in that moment. You need to justify the other character's dialogue if they are describing your emotional state of mind, unless they are clearly making it up and lying. Which would probably be in a parenthetical or written into the action. There is no guesswork here. You need to be like Sherlock Holmes and find the clues to your character. The clues are every-where. Take the time to find them.

WHO AM I RELATING TO?

Know your relationship. Know your history. If you don't have a "face" on each person you are talking to or about, then you are not really talking to or about anyone! The "face" represents someone you know. See that person on the Casting Director's face. Make the Casting Director into the person you're talking to. Feel exactly who that person is to you and you'll be busy dealing with that person and not the Casting Director. It's important to cover this detail because you do not want to have anything or anyone throw you out of a scene.

Make sure you also cover how you relate to each person you're talking to in the scene. How you talk to your father is going to be different from how you talk to your mother, your lover, your brother or your sister. Or how you talk to a cop. What are the dynamics of the relationship? This specific work adds texture, which will separate you out from the masses and get you noticed.

If you are talking about someone, make sure your "someone" is clear to you. Be specific about your relationship.

How do you feel about them? How do you relate to them? However you feel about them and communicate with them will color how you speak about them when you mention their name in the script.

WHAT DO YOU WANT TO MAKE THE OTHER PERSON UNDERSTAND?

Actors have a tendency to act in a vacuum. They act all by themselves by sitting with their own thoughts and feelings without sharing them with anyone. This state causes self-indulgency and inactivity. The end result is that no one will care about you. They'll lose interest and think that you're a boring Actor.

Look, we all want to be heard and understood perfectly. We are all selfish. Think about it, why do we always say, *"You know what I'm saying?" "Right?" "You got it?" "You understand?"* It's because we each want to be heard and we want the other person to get it exactly as we're laying it down.

If you don't make the other person understand what you are saying, then you are going to have no movement or energy in your work. You could be doing some great work, but it's staying inside of you. Throw it at them. Are they listening? Did they really understand it? Did you hear it back how you hear it and not how they said it?

You have to share your emotions. Great acting is when we see someone who is hysterically crying and at the same time making a strong point through the tears. Your point is of utmost importance. All we care about as human beings is making other people understand exactly what we're talking about from our point of view.

So, when you pick up a script and you get excited because you have this great breakdown scene, don't fall in love with it. Fall in love with making the other person understand why you're coming apart at the seams. Keep moving the story along.

Your friend just betrayed you and you're sitting there crying to yourself, *"Oh, I'm feeling betrayed, I'm feeling betrayed!"* Well, who cares unless you lash out at the person that betrayed you and tell your side of the story? If you think of every time that you've felt betrayed, and I know every one of us has felt betrayed on some level, you probably confronted the person or at least told someone how you were betrayed in great detail.

It's got to be about how you are affecting the person with whom you are speaking to, and at the same time, making them understand where you're coming from with every moment, with every line, and with every thought.

WHAT IS YOUR POINT OF VIEW?

If you have two different people with two different points of view, you will never need to find the conflict in the scene. You just need to stick to your point of view. You don't need to find conflict if everyone is doing what they should be doing. For example, he wants to have sex and she needs to finish her paper. That's the conflict. It's that simple. He comes onto her. She doesn't want to do anything because she's preoccupied with a deadline she has for work. She pushes him away. He gets angry. She defends her position. He walks out of the bedroom. He needs to stick to wanting a roll in the hay and she needs to stick to getting her work done or she'll be fired.

Be careful not to pick up the other character's energy and point of view. If you stick to your side of the story, then the other person could be reading it flat, standing on their head chewing bubblegum and farting. It won't matter. Plus, I can assure you, most Casting Directors read fast and flat. Holding strong to your point of view will protect you from their pace and delivery. Go at your own pace.

Just so you know, the reason why most Casting Directors read fast, flat, completely in their page or skip dialogue is because if they were acting with you full out, they wouldn't be able to focus on your work.

Concentrating on your own point of view will also help you with your coverage in Film and Television. Once you get this down, you'll be able to look at a piece of tape on the corner of the camera, which represents your eye line for the other character, with a script supervisor reading the lines of the other character and you will still give a KICK ASS performance. It's all about how your character is feeling and where they're coming from. If you stay on this track, then no one will ever throw you off your game. You will never pick up other people's "stuff" if you stick to your character's point of view.

This is a discipline. It has to be from where your character is coming from. It can never be about you. Leave your ego at home. Don't make random decisions to make it easier for you to play. Figure out where **they** are coming from, relate to it emotionally, and then make your point to the other person.

You need to know how you feel about the other character's point of view, without playing the other character's point of view. You don't need to agree with it, which creates the conflict, but you do need to understand where they are coming from. You never want to be in a guy/guy scene or a girl/girl scene and blend into one person. You never want anyone to switch the parts or to be in the middle of both characters. You need to be a distinct character, with a distinct point of view. You need to represent the person you are playing with all their characteristics in tact.

WHY ARE YOU IN THE SCRIPT?

You might ***just*** be moving the story along. Are you just a Bartender? Are you just a Sushi Chef? Are you just a Factory Worker? If that's who you are, then just do that. Everyone tries to be more than what they're supposed to be. Trust me, you'll stand out if you do what you're supposed to be doing.

You also can't play the whole script in one scene. Ask yourself, in this one scene, what does the Writer want me to be doing? And keep it that simple. You're not supposed to be showing all these colors in one scene. If the breakdown says, "He's broken down, cocky, sexy, cool, vulnerable and wry." What are you going to do? Break down each line including each description? That breakdown is for the entire character for the entire show. Your character might not be all those descriptions in one scene. That's why it never works when Actors read the breakdowns because Actors get confused with how they're going to show all those colors in one scene. Only do what is written. Don't worry about fulfilling the breakdown. It's additional information. Look at the scene as one frame.

Fulfill that one frame. Nothing more - nothing less.

Figure out what you represent in the scene. Ask yourself, "Why did the Writer even write my role? Why am I even there?" In the Television world it's very important to know your place in the script because there are a lot of people who don't book jobs because they're doing too much. They're doing more than the star. In Television, every small role is there to support the lead and the story they're telling. Feature Film is mostly character driven. Every role is important. However, still be careful not to over shoot it. Make sure you represent the character as written.

Be careful about conceptualizing the character. It's very easy to do. When you make choices or you come up with ideas about the character, it'll keep you in concept and in that 99% pile of Actors that do not book. The more you understand who this person is and why they are in the story, the more you'll understand how you're supposed to feel and behave in the situation. If you don't relate to the role on a deep personal level, you will never get into the three-dimensional portrayal of the character. Concept and ideas will keep you outside the material. The more time you spend setting up the life of this character, the more you'll affect your audience. And the more they'll say, "Yeah, that's a real person." It really is that simple.

Take it on in a personal way, take it on in a three-dimensional way, go deep, I mean seriously deep with what is really going on with your character in the story.

A good way not to fall into concept is to come up with adjectives and nouns that would best describe the person in the story that you're going to play. Make a long list with words like "stubborn" or "sneaky" or "wild" or "wacky" and then ask yourself, "When am I this way? How can I relate?"

WHERE ARE YOU?
WHAT TIME OF DAY IS IT?
WHAT'S THE WEATHER LIKE?

The environment (aka "Where Are You?") should never be overlooked simply because the environment will dictate how you will behave, create a stronger illusion and it will keep you safe in the room. If you're in a restaurant having a heated argument with someone, you're not going to be yelling at top of your lungs unless the script indicates it in the parenthetical or in the action. If you're at a ball game, it's going to be difficult to speak with your friend because it's very loud all around you, so you'll probably need to raise your voice. If you're in a courtroom and you're sitting next to your lawyer at the defense table, you're going to want to whisper so that the jurors and the judge won't hear what you're saying. Always adapt your delivery to the environment. This creates the illusion that you are really there.

The environment will also keep you safe in the audition room because you're going to imagine what the place looks like and recreate it. If you have a tendency to pick up energy, hear breathing sounds, wonder why they're not laughing, then your environment isn't strong enough. Let's say that you're on a porch, subsequently you're going to make the "decision makers" in the room the land, the trees, the cows, the barn and the vineyard. It's important to create the entire environment before you walk in the door. The more you can create the illusion of the scene for yourself, the more you'll be busy enough in the audition room to forget who is watching.

"Time Of Day" is another important detail that should never be overlooked. Is it late? How long have you been there? Are there shadows? Is it eerie? Walking into your home alone at 3 AM is way different than walking into your home alone at 11 AM. 3 AM would be a different feeling than 11 AM. At 3 AM you could be more leery of what's behind the door. Time can also give you an indication of where you've been. Let's say that you are on the witness stand and you say that you arrived at the Smith's residence at 2 PM and the crime was committed at 7 AM. That understanding will actually keep your character out of jail. In your mind you will have to know what 2 PM means to you.

"What's The Weather Like?" can affect how you speak. If you're in the South and it's dead summer, you're going to be sweating from the humidity and I'm sure the speed in which you speak will slow down dramatically and you'll be busy patting the sweat off your face. If you're out in the cold stranded standing next to your broken down car on a freeway, you're going to be shivering and moving around to get warm.

All three of these questions ADD TEXTURE and TONE; it literally lifts the illusion of the scene. An Actor is a magician who takes their audience on a magic carpet ride through the illusion, which they create. If your illusion is weak, then your viewing public will not go with you on your journey.

THE 15 GUIDELINES
IN A NUTSHELL

Pick up a script, whether it be commercial or theatrical, sitcom etc., anything at all, stand outside of it and don't make any decisions. Read it like a book 10 times. Pay attention to the punctuation. Don't direct it, act it out or decide on how you're going to play it. Write in one sentence what the story is about. Break down the scene into beginning, middle and end. Find your character's emotional state of mind at the top of the scene because it is 90% of the scene. Map out the emotions of your character in the beginning, middle and end. Find the key line. Circle it, because that's the emotional spine of your character. Read and circle the action to perfect the illusion and to know what you are doing. Know what you are saying in every line. It's all separate thoughts. Pay attention to anything that's in caps, italicized, in quotes or underlined. The Writer wants you to hit it according to how it is written. The more you can personalize what you have to say, the clearer it is to you. The more you understand it, the more we understand it. Don't rush; finish the complete thought. Ask yourself what you are doing in the beginning, middle and end. Find all of your transitions aka mood swings for understanding of character. Ask yourself, *"What is my character's point of view?"* Then, *"How do I hear what the other person is saying?"* Know who the other person is and how you relate to them. Know what you're trying to make the other person understand with your point of view. Figure out why you're in the story so you don't do too much. Know where you are so that the environment will add tone and keep you safe in the room. Know the time of day and the weather so that you can add texture by knowing how to behave given the set up.

When you do all of this, the scene will literally play itself and all you need to do is set it up and take the ride. You need to practice this everyday until the questions become second nature.

THE 10-MINUTE CHEAT SHEET

In one sentence, what is the scene about?

How am I feeling at the top?

When do my feelings change in
the beginning, middle and end?

Where is this for me emotionally?

Who am I dealing with?

How do I feel about them?

What am I doing in the beginning, middle and end?

FINAL THOUGHTS

What will put you into the top 1%? The details! The brilliance is in the details. The details create the moments and the moments create the excitement and interest. Brilliance is striking, distinctive, glittering and bright. In order to book, you must strive for brilliancy.

Always remain humble. Everything that was given to you can just as easily be taken away. The jump in your career can go from hundreds of dollars to hundreds of thousands. Don't forget the people who helped you along the way.

Information is power, folks. Now that you have it, what are you going to do with it?

"The Actor must approach acting like an Olympic Athlete. The more you practice the necessary skills, the more you will book. When a high level of discipline and concentration on the work is achieved, you will see incredible results."

~ Amy Lyndon

™